Animal Purpose

The Hollis Summers Poetry Prize

GENERAL EDITOR: DAVID SANDERS

Named after the distinguished poet who taught for many years at Ohio University and made Athens, Ohio, the subject of many of his poems, this competition invites writers to submit unpublished collections of original poems. The competition is open to poets who have not published a book-length collection as well as to those who have.

Full and updated information is available on the Hollis Summers Poetry Prize web page: ohioswallow.com/poetry_prize

Meredith Carson, *Infinite Morning*
Memye Curtis Tucker, *The Watchers*
V. Penelope Pelizzon, *Nostos*
Kwame Dawes, *Midland*
Allison Eir Jenks, *The Palace of Bones*
Robert B. Shaw, *Solving for X*
Dan Lechay, *The Quarry*
Joshua Mehigan, *The Optimist*
Jennifer Rose, *Hometown for an Hour*
Ann Hudson, *The Armillary Sphere*
Roger Sedarat, *Dear Regime: Letters to the Islamic Republic*
Jason Gray, *Photographing Eden*
Will Wells, *Unsettled Accounts*
Stephen Kampa, *Cracks in the Invisible*
Nick Norwood, *Gravel and Hawk*
Charles Hood, *South × South: Poems from Antarctica*
Alison Powell, *On the Desire to Levitate*
Shane Seely, *The Surface of the Lit World*
Michelle Y. Burke, *Animal Purpose*

Animal Purpose

Poems

Michelle Y. Burke

OHIO UNIVERSITY PRESS

ATHENS

Ohio University Press, Athens, Ohio 45701
ohioswallow.com

Printed in the United States of America
Ohio University Press books are printed on acid-free paper ⊗ ™

26 25 24 23 22 21 20 19 18 17 16   5 4 3 2 1

Library of Congress Cataloging-in-Publication Data
Names: Burke, Michelle Y.
Title: Animal purpose : poems / Michelle Y. Burke.
Description: Athens, Ohio : Ohio University Press, 2016. | Series: The Hollis
  Summers Poetry Prize | Includes bibliographical references.
Identifiers: LCCN 2015045643| ISBN 9780821421987 (pb : alk. paper) | ISBN
  9780821445488 (pdf)
Classification: LCC PS3602.U75527 A36 2016 | DDC 811/.6—dc23
LC record available at http://lccn.loc.gov/2015045643

Acknowledgments

Many thanks to the editors of the following publications, in which these poems, sometimes in different forms and with different titles, first appeared:

American Literary Review: "Not by Extraordinary Means"
Another Chicago Magazine: "Ghost Horse"
The Boiler: "Upon Giving My Grandmother's Chair to My Brother" and
    "Driving Alone"
Georgetown Review: "Pacifisms"
The Hopkins Review: Section 5 of "Homing"
Lake Effect: "Flight Path," "Nocturne," and "Trick of the Light"
The Laurel Review: "Home Economics" and "Sweet Girl"
New Orleans Review: "Zalar's Carousel Horses"
The Offending Adam: "Narcissus"
Parcel: "This Neighborhood"
Poetry: "Diameter" and "Intensity as Violist"
So to Speak: "On the Prospect of Heaven"
Spoon River Poetry Review: "Farmer's Daughter" and "Dear One"
Storyscape: "Horses in Brooklyn"
Waccamaw: "Wishing Stones"

"Driving Alone" was reprinted in *Best of the Net 2014* (Sundress Publications, 2015), "Market Day" was reprinted in *Every River on Earth: Writing from Appalachian Ohio* (Ohio University Press, 2015), and "Dear One" was reprinted in *Deep Waters* (Outrider Press, 2012). "Nocturne" was reprinted in *American Life in Poetry* (2010).

Many thanks to the Dorothy Sargent Rosenberg Memorial Fund, the Cultural Center of Cape Cod, the *American Literary Review*, the Sewanee Writers' Conference, the MacDowell Colony, and the Charles Phelps Taft Research Center for their generous support.

I owe a tremendous debt of gratitude to all my teachers and friends who made this book better. Thanks to James Cummins, Danielle Cadena Deulen, John Drury, Kathy Fagan, Andrew Hudgins, and Lia Purpura, all of whom lead by example. Thanks to Brian Brodeur, Heather Hamilton,

S. Whitney Holmes, Dave Nielson, Natalie Shapero, and Maureen Traverse for their criticism and kindness. Thanks to Thomas Lux for selecting this book for the Hollis Summers Poetry Prize. Thanks to David Sanders and everyone at Ohio University Press. Thanks to Charles Chessler for the use of his photograph. Thanks to my family for their support. Lastly, thanks to Douglas Watson, whose unwavering belief sustains me. Thank you.

for Doug

My Dear One is mine as mirrors are lonely,
As the poor and sad are real to the good king,
And the high green hill sits always by the sea.

—W. H. Auden

Contents

One

Today the Horse

broke from my grip as I led
him from barn to arena. This had
never happened before. I stood
dumbfounded as he galumphed
across the meadow, saddled and bridled,
ducking his head to tear mouthfuls
of spring grass from the field—
the temptation of it all too much
for him. He stepped on his reins,
and I thought, Either the reins will break
or he'll slice his tongue. I watched
as the reins fell in two soft pieces.
I'd stayed out too late drinking
the night before, and I was unprepared
for the sudden rear and heave
of all that horse muscle. At the bar,
I'd been caught up in the gentle
attentiveness with which a friend
brought his ex-wife her ginger ale
and made sure she was happy, holding
the door as she left and asking
if she wanted him to walk her to her car.
At one point, she'd told me
she'd always regretted not going
to medical school. It was what her parents
had wanted, and perhaps the world needed
more doctors who cared about people.
The exes moved around each other
with the quiet assurance of those
who have shared close quarters.

If I could have, I would have wished
that fleeting softness into the world
like pollen that covers everything.
Now the horse was halfway
across the meadow to the hedgerow,
delighted to have the run
of the overgrown field, his bit
turning green from grassy froth,
the remains of his reins curled
like sunning snakes in the long grass.
I approached him slowly, looped half
a rein through his bridle, and led
his thousand pounds back to the barn.
He followed, a frayed strap
of leather between us coordinating
our movements, matching, momentarily,
his animal purpose to mine.

Not by Extraordinary Means

There is so much material   in the material world.

We have no yard; the philodendron pots are small; we'll bury the cat elsewhere.

The Vikings were precise but not extraordinary

in their cruelties. King Ælla's ribs were broken from his spine, then pulled open

behind his back to resemble wings.

                              Little brown bats are vanishing

like smoke from caves they've filled for thousands of years. It is a small thing,

but if you don't add eggs one at a time to cake batter, the emulsion will break,

and the cake won't rise.

                              The Vikings—sometimes they yanked the lungs through.

Salted them.

No, not by extraordinary means, my mother told the doctor when pressed. He wouldn't

let her leave for the night. Then, in her smallest voice, *But, yes, everything else, please.*

First Engagement

There was this Sicilian place.
You had to take the ferry

to get there. Or we did,
living in Brooklyn. The ferry

was free and crowded, but we
elbowed our way to the rail.

Commuters sat inside, drank
beer from the concession stand,

and read the daily news.
We'd gotten engaged,

but we'd call it off soon.
At the Sicilian place,

a woman sat beside us
and ordered every appetizer

on the menu. She told us her cat
was dying. *Baby, Baby is dying.*

Later that night, we argued
by the B61. The word *marriage*

hung in the air like an obscenity.
Nevertheless, I remember staring

into backlit windows,
imagining life unrolling

as smoothly as the stocking
over an actress's leg.

At home, I told our cat
she'd live forever. You said,

Don't give her false hope,
then took your fatalism

to bed. That was the summer
your mother worsened.

Once, toward the end,
she told me to eat the dahlias

before leaving. Whenever
I'm served a salad with flowers—

nasturtiums or marigolds—
I think of that and how

I would have eaten the dahlias
if doing so would have given her

even a little pleasure.

Dear One

The lines on your face grow deeper.
You are more restless each night.
Your dreams are longings
for things forever lost.

Once, I watched a boy's toy pony
slide over the side of a boat.

There's innocence you can't return to
and wouldn't even if the world allowed.
If there are second chances, they come
as metaphor, horses on the backs of waves.

Flight Path

Today I'm reading on our balcony
where I grow wheatgrass for our cat
who's too afraid to come out and eat it
because of the construction noise
emanating from the adjacent warehouse.
This is Brooklyn; even the blue jays
are louder and crankier here.
My husband is reading the *New York Times*,
and I should not interrupt him,
but I want to tell him what a miracle
a pigeon is, how the males produce
crop milk like the females. *Imagine,*
I want to say, *if you could breast-feed!* Last night,
he told me he couldn't think straight
when I left him alone with the cat
because she stared at him as though
he might perform a magic trick
at any moment. He does not like the cat
because he is like the cat, both being,
perhaps, reincarnations of sea sponges.
Lately, I've only been able to read
the Arts section of the *Times* because
the rest is too depressing. In Ohio,
we shared a porch swing and played
a game where one of us offered up
two futures and the other had to choose:
*A great job in Kansas or a lousy one
in New York? A long, amicable marriage
or a short, passionate affair? A house with a porch
or an apartment with a view?* We've chosen

New York, lousy jobs, and a view—
the marriage is still up for grabs. People
like to ask questions they already know
the answers to, like the elderly woman
at the farmers' market who keeps asking,
Is this fresh? On weekends, my husband indulges
my desire to sleep with the blinds up; I like
to be awakened by the sun. From our balcony,
we watch planes cut white lines in the sky.

A Life

Each afternoon he took his pipe
and led his goats beyond the pasture
to a neighbor's field behind his farm—
not exactly his but not exactly not.

As the goats clipped the tall grasses,
he sat in the chair he never failed
to bring. Sometimes he read, most often
not. The vetch climbed the goldenrod,

the dandelions turned from gold
to globe, and every day he went,
thinking to himself how good it was
to be almost but not entirely alone.

Horses in Brooklyn

I was on my way to pick up vegetables
which are delivered each week
as though by a miracle
from a local farm to my favorite bar
when I passed a small herd of horses —
if six or seven makes a herd.
They were hitched to the side of a trailer
pulled up along the sidewalk.
The block was closed,
policemen stood at the corners,
and someone shoveled manure.
The horses didn't care.
Each stood with its head down,
weight distributed among three legs,
the fourth cocked at the fetlock,
making them look sassy.
They were acting horses
brought in for a television miniseries
about a Harlem hospital
at the turn of the century.
It was being filmed in Greenpoint,
also known as Little Poland.
The miniseries would deal
in a provocative way with race,
I was told by the man shoveling manure.
It's hard to say anything meaningful
about race, he continued, but he wasn't saying
the attempt shouldn't be made.
Two horses were led away,
hitched to a buggy,

and directed to trot up and down
the dirt-covered street.
After they halted and the driver hopped down,
the horse on the left
strained against his harness,
craned his neck,
and gnashed his teeth
in his partner's face.
This was a more honest expression
of *horse*, I suppose,
than the beautiful unison achieved
while the camera rolled.

Pacifisms

Before going to bed, I read an article
about Camus, then wake to find my cat
chewing stitches from her belly.
On hold with the vet, I remember
something clever the article writer said—
that Camus did not ask the liberal
question *How do we make tomorrow
better than today?* but the grander question
Why not kill yourself tonight?
My cat's eleven. Before long, I'll choose
between treatment and palliative care,
but today, I haul her fifteen pounds
down the stairs and into my Nissan,
resenting the instinct that tells her
to pull threads from her abdomen,
to lick the incision until it bleeds.
The vet assures me that this is all
to be expected, that cats are stitched
on the inside as well as the out.
Later, on the phone with my husband,
I mean to tell him about Camus,
but instead I tell the story of a man
I once knew who caught an owl thieving
in his henhouse. He'd grabbed her
with gloved hand and held her upside down
until she went limp, wings spreading
like a crucifix. I had seen chickens do this
but never something wild. At dawn,
he walked the hill he lived on, showing her
to everyone, saying, *This owl*

has been stealing my chickens. Look at her!
The owl, he said, was mortified.
He walked to the top of the hill
and looked into her nearly closed eyes.
He whispered, *I could have killed you,*
but I didn't. Then he opened his hand.

Two

On the Prospect of Heaven

Growing up, I believed in salvation
and my mother's definition of heaven:
A place containing everything

I'd ever wanted. What I wanted
was a pony. A real one. I had plastic ones
with rainbows and butterflies

on their rumps. They had stripper names
like Cotton Candy and Butterscotch.
If you are good, my mother said,

you'll go to heaven. And get a pony,
I added. It seemed fair.
Death + Goodness = Pony.

But at church, the priest said goodness
was the absence of sin, and this
confused me. You can't go about

making an absence. It's there
or it isn't, and really, if you stumble
into one, you've negated it.

Inchworm

I want to confess
I'm a little in love with Pope Francis
and his refusal to wear red shoes.
(Mother, it's not a sin.)
I like to imagine him taking
the red shoes out
when no one's looking
and hefting the solid leather in his palm.
He doesn't intend (of course)
to slip them on
but then—what could it hurt?
Just to see. Once,
when I felt magnanimous,
I bought tickets to a fashion show
and invited my mother.
I told her to wear black.
(Mother, you should wear black
more often.)
Isn't it strange how every person
you know was once a different person,
a younger one,
and you can't go back
and meet that other person now,
and this is a reason for sadness
but a small one? At sixteen, my mother
attended modeling school
at her local department store.
(I had no idea.)
At the fashion show,
she was the expert: *Look how they slant.*

When they walk, they place their feet
as though on a tightrope.
Their arms are behind their bodies.
Here, try. No, really, pull
your shoulders back. Back!
My mother too (I suspect)
is in love with Pope Francis
and also with Bill Clinton,
which is why my father is a Republican.
I don't believe in miracles,
but every day this week
I've pulled an inchworm
from my geranium, and I look
and don't see any more,
but the next day—another inchworm.
Holy inchworm, patron saint
of nonbelievers, pray for us.
We are easily beguiled.

Sweet Girl

Such a sweet girl
is just another way of saying,
Not too bright but someone you'd trust
with your dog.

And *cuteness*, I'm told,
has to do with the size of one's eyes
relative to one's head.

My husband, for example,
says I have a small head,
and this accounts largely
for my charm.

The truth is, I have dog-sat
for dozens of people and, once,
lugged a dying Irish setter

up and down multiple stairs,
so he could pee
by his favorite pine, then sleep curled
on his master's bed.

Tears, this morning's paper
tells me, can lower a man's
testosterone level.

Look, I want to say,
it's like the way out of the fight
is in the fight.

The Irish setter—he died a week later.

Saints and Martyrs

At age nine, I announced I wasn't a virgin.

I didn't know what the word meant,
but I knew Mary was one,
and Mary was good, and I wasn't, not really.

I'm told my mother consulted Dr. Spock
and her psychiatrist about this.

During confession, I made things up
to please the priest,
wanting him to like me.

I still do this, but not with priests.

Our church was called St. Rose of Lima.
There were saints and martyrs everywhere,
pierced by arrows, bludgeoned
with stones, broken on wheels.

They bled and looked heavenward.

The priest explained, We honor the martyrs
not because of how they lived
but because of how they died.

Lives of the Artists

We gazed at portraits of dancers
tugging on ballet shoes, women at the bath
twisting to touch some obscure point
on the back, and brothel scenes
in which whores scratched at derrieres,
and I imagined Degas at the brothel,
stiff-backed in a brocade chair,
goatee vaginal about his mouth,
sketchbook against knee, pencil scribbling
back and forth, charcoal dust in the air.

The only time I'd been to Paris,
I was twenty-one and spent a night
with a young man named Baptiste.
We talked about God until dawn,
and then he ran out for croissants
and coffee. I threw open the shutters
of the old hotel room and watched
the early light crawl up the ornate plaster
of the opposing row house.
I kissed him good-bye like an angel.

I'd never told you about Baptiste.
It's difficult to explain, just as
it's both true and untrue that Degas
went to the brothel for *art*.
As we left the museum, you reminisced
about a woman you once loved.
You said, *She was pretty but not beautiful,
a writer but not an artist,* all of which
was intended to ease my anxiety,
and—I'm ashamed to admit—it did.

Home Economics

They tried the usual remedies—
lace garters, salted baths, chairs up against the wall,
unusual places.

Scarcity creates demand, he said, and then,
It's just that you're always here now.

This isn't economics, she said, touching the lace
of her new silk panties.

Flood Zone

At Coney Island, we ate funnel cake
loaded with confectioners' sugar and watched
the moon rise like an orange over the sea.
I tried hard not to think of another time
we'd stood by the sea, when you and your brothers
cast ashes against waves, so I talked
about an article I'd recently read—
the story of a man who rode the Cyclone.
He'd walked off fine, a numbness in his hands,
a pain in his neck, but four days later—dead.
The braking system failed, I said, allowing
the coaster to reach unsafe speeds. Last year,
we'd ridden the same coaster. I'd coaxed you
into it. *Come on. It'll be fun.* You complained
about back pain later, but I laughed, believing
everything was fine, always would be.

That night we saw teens haul a lifeguard's chair
beyond the surf and use it as a diving board.
That's about the dumbest thing I've ever seen,
you said. Then I said something equally dumb
about the glory of risk and how it makes one feel
more alive to brush the fringes of death,
to pass near the curtain without going through.

Weeks later, we walked the India Street pier
and watched the ferry crisscross the East River
as the sun set behind the city. Buildings came alive
with lights, and I imagined men and women
turning off computers and stacking papers

as others gathered buckets and mops and began
their night. On the pier, men reeled in fishing line
and dogs sniffed at buckets in which fish circled.
The sun sank behind a band of clouds,
and for just a moment, the light broke through
and arranged itself into perfect rays. Crisp and clean,
they shot upward until lost in the greater blue.

Here

My agonies were over things like brunches,
    exes, and the black box of your heart
where you courted lovers from twenty years ago.
    So we followed a script of skepticism,

throwing in a bit of—what? Me, standing along a fence,
    forehead pressed against chain link, watching
you hit a backhand volley down the line;
    you drinking lemonade on my porch swing

as I freed peonies from winter detritus;
    mornings when you were up before me
and brought me coffee in bed then sat in sunlight,
    watching me drink; a night when your mother

slept downstairs, the cancer filling her lungs,
    and we—I swear—felt God enter the room.
Even now, I'm amazed to find us together,
    waiting on subway platforms in Brooklyn,

guessing which way the next train is coming
    by its preceding wind. So often we're late,
rushing into theater seats seconds before
    the curtain's drawn. Do you remember

when I cried at the end of As You Like It
    because you didn't think to hold my hand?
How many allegations, apologies,
    and midnight monologues have brought us here?

I look back and am certain there's nothing
    to explain our late-rushed arrival
except an underground system more efficient
    than anything we might have planned.

Three

Homing

1. *Live Pigeon Shoot*

The pigeon I scoop from his carrier
holds within his breast two shotgun pellets

lodged too deep to be removed.
I've worked on farms and slaughtered chickens,

but what gets me about this pigeon shoot
is that while some raised rifles in the air

and aimed at birds released from cages,
others waited, then gathered the wounded birds

and brought them to the nearest wildlife rehab
center, this one, in Manhattan, where now

a vet-in-training treats the wounds, or when
it seems best to her, euthanizes.

The proximity of these actions—
the destruction of life for pleasure

and the insistence that *all life* is precious—
reminds me that I understand little

about the world. I, too, am selfish
in regard to pleasure, rarely providing

my husband with the favors that would please
him so much and cost me so little.

Yet here I am on Sunday morning,
holding down a pigeon, spreading the feathers

on its chest. The vet injects vitamin K
into the muscle that runs along the breastbone.

I don't know how to gentle the world,
but some of the tamest horses I've ridden

were those trained with the firmest hand.

2. *Beginning with a First Line from Larkin*
        April 15, 2013

On the day of the explosion,
sunshine crashed between the buildings;
running water rinsed the remnants

of last night's dinner from the dishes.
Reporters spoke in confusion,
threads of knowledge spooling out of them,

filling up our living room and kitchen.
At four, you called from midtown's tower,
saying you hadn't heard from your brother —

he lived in Boston, worked downtown.
And so the spider of information
spewed its content in all directions

but never gave us what we wanted.
Turning back to the dishes,
water drowning out the voices,

I thought what thoughts I thought alone.

3. *After the Pigeon Shoot*

Juana works with the calm of a mother
who understands intuitively
what must be done. She doesn't need to be asked
or instructed but under fluorescent lights

moves from sink to cage to steel counter,
bundling, feeding, and cleaning, now singing
again her Spanish song, each pigeon
a memory of a child she once sang to.

The pigeons settle peacefully
into her palms and open their beaks, and she
ladles the moistened puppy kibble in.
While I, not yet a mother, fumble

with each pigeon, prying its beak
open and pushing the kibble in,
and there's no grace in what I do,
only efficiency, which is what

I have to offer. When a vet asks me
to clear mucus from a sick bird's throat,
I do, but I'm disgusted by
the bloody strands left on the cotton swab.

After receiving the hospital's report
on her mother's death, my mom read it to me
on the phone, an edge in her voice that meant
she blamed the hospital. She believed

in the competence of science to stave off
the end. It is nearly impossible
to embody competence and gentleness
at once. Since her mother's death, my mom

has waded out into the sea of her own gentleness.
She talks to the cardinals and squirrels
that eat the seed she places each morning
on the table outside her window.

Even the dog in my mom's house is lonely,
standing each afternoon by the fence,
watching the neighbor dogs frolic.
A person can spend her whole life

at the window, peering in, wondering why
she wasn't invited to the party,
but a dog will wait, wagging its tail,
expecting any moment to be let in.

4. After Auden

April 16, 2013

About acts of violence they can never agree,
husbands and wives: how long they talk
under covers at night, rehashing the day's events
only to be tired at work the next day and no wiser.

At a coffee shop in Brooklyn, men and women
in T-shirts and caps tap at keyboards. When a man
in paint-spattered pants walks in, the barista asks,
What are you working on today? He replies,
The giant woman. Outside, the Creative Landscaping
and Paving Company jackhammers the sidewalk,
measuring progress by the growing debris,
and the barista says, *I'll have to rethink my playlist.*

In California, your brother vacations.
Yesterday, he surfed, and his wife snapped pictures,
sending them to Brooklyn. They had no idea
that shrapnel had shredded the legs of runners and bystanders
back home. In the photos, they take turns squinting into the sun,
shielding their eyes so they can smile.

5. *Homing*

Jack tells me his brother refused
to buy a house after he waved
a voltage meter about the place
and discovered a strong electromagnetic
field in the room that would have been
his daughter's. I've read that a pigeon
released 500 miles from home at dawn
can fly back by dusk and this
has something to do with particles
in the pigeon's head and the earth's
magnetic field. Jack now sleeps on a mat
embedded with electrical wires;
he plugs it into the wall. *Grounded*, he says.
I learn that we — electrical beings —
walk around unable to dissipate

our potential, and so, for one week,
I give a dollar to everyone who asks for one
on the subway and monitor my state
to see if this makes me feel better
or worse. Inconclusive.

                    All of the starlings
in North America are descendants
of those brought here in the 1800s
by the American Acclimatization Society
to fill Central Park with every species
mentioned in Shakespeare. The native species
were outcompeted, changing the ecosystem
irrevocably. A saw-whet owl sheltering
in the cedar closes his eyes and fades
into the bark. Once, in a cabin in the woods,
I opened my eyes the way a leafless tree
senses the lengthening of days and found
a juvenile deer sunlit and still on my porch.
It shivered at the edges of its being
like a blossoming cherry tree.

                              The unexpected
grace of the world undoes me at times as when
a woman appears at the wildlife rehab center
with a shoebox of opossums in hand.
She saw the mother hit by a taxi,
checked the pouch, and pulled out twelve
barely furred babies, now nestled
in the fleece that lines their shoebox.
When I place my hand inside, they snuffle
and lean into my warmth.

                        Jack insists
he sleeps better on his mat. I ask if he

believes in the whole electromagnetic thing—
not the physical force but the supposed
therapeutic effects—and he says no,
but, being the child of two psychologists,
he does believe in the placebo effect.

6. *Kingdom of Compromise*

We do again and again what gives us pain.
Adulthood, kingdom of compromise.
We have the same argument day after day.

Some days are difficult to explain,
children expecting us to affirm or deny.
We do again and again what gives us pain.

There are questions that refuse to be weighed.
Parents and politicians improvise
the same argument day after day.

At what point does death become humane?
When suffering cannot be stopped otherwise?
Again and again, we weigh others' pain.

The world offers itself *as is*, no claim
of fairness, sense, or adequate supply.
It makes no argument beyond the day.

To bend events into stories that stay
is one of the ways we apologize.
We keep doing what gives us pain,
facing the same argument day after day.

7. Homing (II)

The day of my wedding, I walked into a stable
where two horses ate, their long faces
swinging up to take me in. Deciding
I offered nothing better, they returned
to the serious business of chewing.
In the fragrant air, they were sleek machines.
Their owner, a burly and talkative man
who'd nailed a sack of carrots to the wall,
said, *Look at that. Scout's bitten Gingersnap*
on the neck again. He pulled a jar of ointment
from a shelf and smeared it on the half-moon bite.
Gingersnap continued her mastication,
flicking her ears a few times in annoyance.
I'll have to separate them again, he said,
gesturing toward Gingersnap, then Scout,
sighing to signal what trouble it was
to love such incorrigible beasts.

What does it mean that in marriage
we give our bodies to one another?
Could any gift be more dreadful?
On our honeymoon in Sicily, my husband
and I joked: With his bum leg and my
sensitive stomach, we would have been left
on the mountainside in ancient times
or abandoned in the woods to be devoured,
our bellies soft fruit for the lions.
On our return flight to LaGuardia, we watched
the Frenchwoman in 23B
swill red wine heartily until, an hour
before landing, she fingered the flight
attendant's tie and said, *Oh, dear, could you*
bring me a bit of water? which he did

as she smoothed her sailor-boy blouse.
Unrumpled, she turned to me and said,
Ah, with service like that, who needs first class?
The wine had stained the corners of her mouth.

Perhaps love is fiercest when you suspect
that no one would love your beloved as you do.
My mother, for example, grew strident
in her love for her mother when the latter
was in her 90s and mean to everyone.
Perhaps we fear the loss of the groomed self
we present to the world. Or perhaps
we can't really believe we're lovable at all,
and so we throw our love against the edges
of the world to witness how it flows
into the crevices, soft and smooth as honey.

8. *Long View*

On one of the last warm days of autumn,
we sailed a catboat into Boston Harbor
and looked back at the city from the water.
We couldn't hear the buzz of all that living

from our floating wooden casket, bobbing
up and down upon the busy water.
That's always how it is, I thought. *The near
drowns out the far no matter how you strain.*

Then one clear siren rose up from the city
and winged its way across the water,
drawing our attention back to the living,
leaving its cry unanswered in the air.

Four

Puff

First it's me weeping, listening
to the Moth Radio Hour, and some cop's
talking about his dog being hit
by a car and holding the dog
on the way to the vet and seeing the moment
the last puff of breath goes out.
Then it's you crying because it's hard
to find meaning in copyediting
and we're trying to make a baby
and failing. Everyone knows that most
of the world's blogs balled up together
wouldn't equal one *New Yorker* piece,
but—puff—there goes another magazine
collapsing like a house of cards.
One becomes a bit sentimental
about print and by one I mean me.
Two hundred years ago, there were ferries
powered by horses. My father-in-law
tells me the horses were blinded
so they wouldn't go mad treading the same
dark circle each day. I can easily accept
the fact of ferries—tons of metal and wood
floating—but it's hard to imagine those horses,
hooves the size of dinner plates,
suspended only by physics and water.

Dante Park

Dante, I have known you only in translation
and incompletely, which is perhaps all
I can say of my knowledge of anyone
or anything, but I am glad to see you
when I walk down Broadway on my way to buy
slacks at a store I despise but which sells them
in a size I can wear without hemming.
I admire your resolute stare, the way you ignore
the dancers and musicians in the halls to the west.
Perhaps you are thinking of *literature*. Perhaps
you are wondering why your park is so small.

At Martin Luther King Jr. High School,
I watched a teacher guide his students
through the labyrinthine syntax of the *Inferno*.
Halfway through class, two cops
came into the room and led a girl away.
No one objected, no one *moved* when they
took that girl away.

                    Would it comfort you,
Dante, to know that students are being taught
your *Inferno*? It's even been made into a video game.
On the radio this morning, a man in his fifties
with Parkinson's said that over one hundred
billion people have died in all of human history.
That's a lot of souls. How many have read
your *Inferno*? Millions? Alas, few make it
all the way through *Purgatorio* to *Paradiso*.

Narcissus

1.

Daffodils reproduce sexually *and* asexually. How lovely to have options.

Also, the Latin name for a daffodil is Narcissus.

Narcissus the man fell in love with himself then killed himself because his love

    could not be reciprocated.

The gods, they were always springing whole from one another's foreheads

    and thighs, but the humans, they could only conceive thigh on thigh,

    the surprise in their eyes mirrored in the eyes of another.

2.

A thing should be one thing or another. Not both/and. Not God *and* human.

Inside my body there is one heart beating seventy beats per minute and another

    beating one hundred and forty.

Like if you cracked open a chocolate bunny and found another chocolate bunny inside,

    only smaller and with a faster heartbeat.

Like if you draw a circle big enough any one piece of it viewed closely

    would resemble a line. At some point would become a line.

Ghost Horse

Impossible now to abandon the world   no leave-taking

no unseen custodian sweeping up behind you   no snowdrift of responsibility

piling up elsewhere   you thought it might come to this

now you know how responsibilities change you   not like when you were young

and whispered fidelities into the ears of others   —some you have even kept—

no, this is a horse charging across a meadow   you could run but the horse

can run faster   better to brace for impact or believe the horse

might pass right through   your molecules aligned

one constellation threading another   you learned about this once in school

eighth-grade physics   how physical objects are mostly empty air

then you threw a tennis ball at a wall for hours   waiting to see it disappear

what you can't know now   is that this horse *will* pass right through

and when it does   it will seize every fidelity you've ever had

you'll spend your whole life running after   begging the horse

to drop them, to leave them on the ground   like sticks bereft of leaves.

This Neighborhood

provides shelter for the strays but last night
a homeless man froze to death in the park
where on Sundays I buy almond butter
and spelt bread, the park where in the spring
my husband and I watch the pigeons court.
The old Polish men speak only Polish
and go only to the shelter where the workers
speak Polish, but it's been closed because of
resistant neighbors.

           Last night I went to hear
a poet I love. She's in her 90s and has suffered
several strokes and the words leave her sometimes
as when nearing the end of her reading,
she wanted to let us know the end was near
and said, *This will be the last of these things.*
The last . . . group of words.

           Earlier, she kept turning
aside a paper and finding on the paper beneath
another of her poems. She smiled in recognition
as though encountering by chance an old friend.
She said, mostly to herself, *Oh, yes, this is a good one.*
Oh, I remember you—delighted to be stumbling across
these earlier versions of herself.

           It is something
worth striving for maybe that when later we come
upon these earlier selves, we think, *Oh, yes,*
this is a good one. Oh, I remember you.

Driving Alone

At Lake Erie, the sky collapsed
in snow. My headlights lit up
a miniature globe before me, a world
too small to navigate.

What does it mean when the only
signs we have of others
are the lights they send out?
I made it somewhere safely.

Or safely made it somewhere.
I can't remember how. Who knows
what we pass unseen.

Upon Giving My Grandmother's Chair
to My Brother

It's a good chair,
heavy wooden frame,
stripes with sailboats inside them,
comfortable slab of a cushion.
I remember reading Ovid
in Ohio in this chair.
I remember when the old couple
turned into trees,
leaves sprouting from their lips,
just enough time to say farewell.
From this chair I could see
the man in the apartment
across the alley
on nights he left his blinds up.
Sometimes he read too,
each of us alone
in our own orb of light.

Trick of the Light

In France, the pickpockets
ask tourists to sign petitions
against social injustice,
then run their hands over
their intimate belongings,
gentle and needy as lovers.
It's hard to judge them harshly,
such artistry.
Even the rush-hour crowd
hurrying toward the downtown C
parts for the woman in checkered spandex
twirling a hula-hoop about her waist
while standing on her head.
Dear unobservant god,
do not snuff us out.
We are beautiful and strange.

Zalar's Carousel Horses

The eyes of a Zalar horse always have a certain sadness to them.

—*Tobin Fraley*

The best ones—not dictated
but revealed—are mostly
gone. See how they hardly

resist the rain. Horse
replaced by horsepower.
How much goes

unchanged? The earnestness
of an eagle carved
in a horse's chest.

Zalar, the Michelangelo
of horse carvers. Did he know
what his horses

carried, how sorrow
manifests itself
in wood, how art,

unlike duty,
reveals desire
and its afterimage,

loss? Today,
a fiberglass-cast cavalry
parades through theme parks

and midways. Gears
imitate the gallop, and we
salvage what we can:

rivets carved in armor,
a neck bathed in roses,
a wild, upturned head.

Five

Market Day

The sky is clear tonight. The plow horses
stand silent in the field, and the wife calls
to her husband to bring the truck around:
Tomorrow is market day, and the lettuces
must be packed in the cool night hours.

If their vegetables are flawless, they can ask
a high price, so they swaddle their lettuces
in burlap and stack the crates carefully.
When the truck is loaded, the wife follows
her husband up the stairs to the bedroom

they'd built to be a hayloft back when
there was still going to be a house. At dawn,
she'll rise, go downstairs, and milk the goats
she calls by name. She'll drive away, leaving
for her husband's coffee a single jar of milk.

Nocturne

A man can give up so much,
can limit himself to handwritten correspondence,
to foods made of whole grains,
to heat from a woodstove, logs
hewn by his own hand and stacked neatly
like corpses by the back door.

He can play nocturnes by heart.
They will not make his beloved appear.
He can learn the names of all the birds
in the valley. Not one
will be enticed to learn his.

Last Light

The sky layered like a trifle,
the sand giving back
the sun's final hue.
Eliot plays in the sand.
He borrows a shovel
from a bigger boy.
For minutes, they work
in undefined unity,
relocating sand
from point A
to B. The sun
disappears. Fog
rolls in, escalator smooth.
The bigger boy asks
for his shovel back.
Eliot, two, refuses.
There is an eruption
of tears, Eliot hefted
like a sack of laundry
by his mother.
So the days go—
blessed, mundane—
until God points a finger
at your chest and says,
Now everything must change.

Diameter

You love your friend, so you fly across the country to see her.

Your friend is grieving. When you look at her, you see that something's missing.

You look again. She seems all there: reading glasses, sarcasm, leather pumps.

What did you expect? Ruins? Demeter without arms in the British Museum?

Your friend says she believes there's more pain than beauty in the world.

When Persephone was taken, Demeter damned the world for half the year.

The other half remained warm and bountiful; the Greeks loved symmetry.

On the plane, the man next to you read a geometry book, the lesson on finding

    the circumference of a circle.

On circumference: you can calculate the way around if you know the way across.

You try *across* with your friend. You try *around*.

I don't believe in an afterlife, she says. *But after K. died, I thought I might go after her.*

    In case I'm wrong. In case she's somewhere. Waiting.

Intensity as Violist

That she was not pretty she knew.

The flowers delivered into her hands post-concert by the young girl, pretty,

    would be acknowledged only. To display was to invite comparison.

Skilled at withholding, she withheld; it was a kind of giving.

As when meditation is a kind of action,

a way of leaning into music the way one leans into winter wind,

the way a mule leans into a harness,

the way a lover leans into the point of deepest penetration.

After a ship's prow cuts the water, the water rushes back twice as hard.

Farmer's Daughter

If it were easy, she says, and the blade,
in mid-arc, stills, *I'd stop*, and the bird's neck,

a snowy thing, bloodies. *Come here*, she says,
and I do. *I'll show you something beautiful.*

She peels back warm flesh, and there,
nestled in fat, eggs. The moment is tenuous

as a lacewing landing on a pea shoot, stark
as a steer skull uncovered by rain. Because

all poems about death are love poems.
Because later we'll soak up blood with hay.

Around here nothing goes to waste.
She slides her hand inside the bird.

This part's easy, she says and wraps her fingers
around the heart, pulls. What's surprising

is how hard it is, how much a muscle.
The gizzard she cuts in half.

Inside, there are stones. *Without stones,*
she says, *they'll die. If they need to,*

they'll eat their eggs. Because I want
to hold back her hand and say, *This one,*

this one shall live. The meat birds—
we never named them, though Brewster

flapped free and lived to eat bread crumbs
thrown from the farmhouse door.

In her ease of motion, in her strength,
I saw an unwillingness to believe

weakness could be a virtue. *Come here,*
eat this stone. Against it, whet your heart.

Wishing Stones

Sometimes I wish we were the calm expanse
    of a clear, wooden desk.

Sometimes I wish we were the spider's abdomen
    silhouetted against the moon.

Sometimes I wish we were the mole,
    who tunnels underground,
        who places his small, breakable back
            so eagerly beneath the earth.

Notes

"Pacifisms": The quotations are from Adam Gopnik, "Facing History," A Critic at Large, *New Yorker*, April 9, 2012.

"Homing": Section 2 begins with the first line of Philip Larkin's poem "The Explosion" in *Collected Poems* (2004). Section 4 begins with a paraphrase of the opening of W. H. Auden's poem "Musée des Beaux Arts" in *Selected Poems* (2007).

"On the Prospect of Heaven": Suggested by Mark Strand's "Keeping Things Whole" in *Reasons for Moving* (1980).